Six Rivers

Six Rivers

Jenna Le

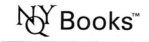

The New York Quarterly Foundation, Inc.
New York, New York

NYQ Books™ is an imprint of The New York Quarterly Foundation, Inc.

The New York Quarterly Foundation, Inc.
P. O. Box 2015
Old Chelsea Station
New York, NY 10113

www.nyqbooks.org

First Edition

Set in New Baskerville

Layout and Design by Raymond P. Hammond
Cover Illustration by Austin Allen

Library of Congress Control Number: 2011931653

ISBN: 978-1-935520-46-7

Six Rivers

Acknowledgments

The following poems first appeared in the following magazines: "Inheritance," *Salamander;* "Ethnography," "The Pickled Womb," "Vespers," *Minnetonka Review;* "The Apprentice Pearl-Divers," "Venetian Blinds," "Art Lessons," *Reflexions;* "The Shortest Memoir," *Yemassee;* "Tire Swing," *Journal of Medical Humanities;* "A Correspondence," "The Day Before All the Names Changed," *New York Quarterly;* "The Harvard Square Street Musicians," "Salisbury," *Post Road;* "Troubadour's Song," *Barrow Street;* "Lobster," *The Gamut;* "Haibun," *Modern Haiku;* "The Cannibals Will Inherit the Earth," *Ellipsis;* "Three Short Poems on a Common Theme," *Rhino;* "Hymn to Aphrodite," *Margie;* "Marsyas," *Raintown Review.*

Contents

The Aorta

The River Styx

And all these rivers converged on a great marsh...

The Perfume River

(Hue, Vietnam)

MOM'S COCKS

Mom grew up beside the Perfume River in Vietnam,
in a brick house overrun by chickens.
Those horny-footed fowl were always
rubbing their feather-padded genitals
against sofa legs and children's shoes
as if they were fit to burst. Mom laughs

as she tells me how they ground
their pelvises against her leather sandal,
stuporous with misdirected lust—
How strange that she
is talking to me about sex
in this casual way. She's returning to her roots

as a child who lived among
unmannered beasts. And I, through hearing her words,
am returning there with her: I
am the aggressive rooster; I'm the hens
cowering behind the outhouse; I'm the much-abused,
much-abraded, Size Four shoe.

INHERITANCE

the dead
who gave me life
give me this
　　　—Lorine Niedecker

I have my ancestors to thank
for the skin between my stretch marks:
the yellow-tinged and paper-thin covering
that I wear on my gregarious cheeks and in
my secret armpits.

No other heirlooms have lasted.
Nothing else tangible, nothing else that mists
when, despite your awe, you breathe on its
semiprecious surface. Only my yellow body fits
the bill.

I have last century's warmongers
to thank for this sorry fact:
politicians, children trained to kill,
and an ocean, stormy-yellow-black.

ETHNOGRAPHY

Females of our tribe
lack beauty: scrubby tomboys
with uneven teeth.

Our eyes are perfect
zeroes, designed for looking
and not being seen.

Scrawny yellow efts
that bask on bare rocks and soak
up sunlight, we are

cold-blooded beasts; we
constantly need refueling,
constantly need touch,

need warm hands palming
our moist skin. Need to be kept
alive, not admired.

THE APPRENTICE PEARL-DIVERS

Bright as your eyes are, they are less bright
than the eyes of the apprentice who misguessed
how long a lanky boy with a narrow chest
can hold his breath on a pearl dive. Hot nights,
his ghost still slinks among the village bunks,
beds of the boys who were his friends; lifting the cloths
that overlie their naked flanks,
he spanks them, teasingly scolding them for sloth.

At breakfast the next day, they're too afraid
to speak of what they saw: a boy, long-dead,
whose ardent eyes seared holes in their chaste sleep.
Uneasily they stand and cross themselves,
troop to church in trembling groups of ten or twelve,
and, when the priest expounds on angels, weep.

1. A boy dives and dies and then they
   have a funeral the next day
2. 2 stanzas, no rhyme scheme. but
   some lines rhyme
3. 1st line is pretty pos. but by the
   end it is pretty sad
4. 1st Stanza: Line 8
   2nd Stanza: Line 6

16

COMPANION

How explain the blondish eyelash
afloat in my cooling oolong?
There must be a ghost, invisible except
for his yellow facial hair,
sharing my house, squatting in my chair.

Not brazen enough to sip from my cup, though.
He's shy; he breathes soundlessly—
none of that pinball clatter
tuberculous lungs make.
(He must have died for love's sake.)

He'd rather go hungry—he's used to that—
than wantonly paw around
in my silverware drawer. Is it a kosher thing?
Yet he doesn't scruple
to borrow my razor to banish his stubble.

That blade nicked my skin once,
and our two bloods mingled.
In that moment, I caught his disease:
I'm now part ghost,
fearful of loam, famished for tea and toast.

TRIOLET (SAIGON, 1980)

Mister, can you tell me where I can find
a bedmate for a yellow-toothed, yellow-skinned girl?
In her thirty years, she has never drunk white wine.
Mister, can you tell me where I can find
a replacement for the sister who used to twine
round her body as she slept, knees tightly curled?
Mister, can you tell me where I can find
a bedmate for a yellow-toothed, yellow-skinned girl?

The Mississippi River

(Minneapolis, Minnesota)

THE SHORTEST MEMOIR

Back when my breasts and two-piece bathing suit were new,
I'd take walks on the shore where the rabbit traps sprung.
And the breeze would lick my ribs with its raw wet tongue
like a hungry Southern boy at a barbecue.

1. ABBA rhyme schemes, & southern curry
   2 lines

2. Seems positive and as a memory as
   one misses those days and puts
   across tone of the poem

3. The pictures are circles at the
   beach then at a BBQ

4. Spring

5. The rhyme goes nicely and the way
   the poem is set up reads well

6. I like it because it reminds me
   of the beach and the food people
   have so it creates a personal
   connection

EARLY DAYS

Purring, Dad's car stalked
the rat-tailed American dream
Its vibrations shook the cradle where I dozed

Till he returned at nightfall,
our house pocketed his absence
like an apple whose theft is to be regretted

My big sister, 7 years old,
had a large flaring mouth
like a lion or a trumpet

My mother said: Surely my older daughter
will grow up to be a storyteller

I was the stubborn, shifty kid
on whom she liked to tell tales

TRICK

America, you're
the Halloween costume
my immigrant father
rented and never returned.

Dad clambered inside
your baggy interior
because he wanted his share
of the season's sweet treats.

With your reptilian tail,
Dad batted away
his rivals and scampered
on to his goal.

Dressed up in you,
my father seduced
my starry-eyed mother
behind a tall hedge.

But now the costumier
is demanding you back.
He calls our house daily,
ringing the phone off its hook.

PIANO TEACHER

You're enclosed with him—
                              an albino man and his piano—
in a small soundproofed room
in a labyrinth of underground rooms. You're a virgin, all right;
the Minotaur's labyrinth
is just the place for you.

The dim-watted electric lights
flicker. Their buzz is the snoring
of a negligent babysitter.
How shortsighted the grown-ups were
to abandon you to this fate!

The unevenly yellowed, sticky keys,
an inferior plastic:
how many Band-Aid-looped fingers
have scraped their surfaces?

The hairs on the backs of his hands are glassy, erect.
He stretches his arms across yours to reach the low keys,
to prove a point. Is that his armpits you smell?
And is he the Phantom of the Opera?

You rent him by the hour. He lectures you
on "the Romantics," and his pale-lashed eyes squeeze shut
when the music you make makes him dizzy.
By now, you know his hands better than your dad's—
arched and muscular—a vulture's horny feet.

TIRE SWING

Rubber tire, you once were wed to a workaholic wheel;
when he divorced you, you tried to hang yourself
from a tree branch;
now you cradle a child in the curve
of your rugged arm.

A CORRESPONDENCE

Your latest postcard gloated: "The Barcelona sun
casts an estrous glow over the red clay roofs.
It inspires stray dogs
to make love in the streets: why, just last night,

our own well-bred Claudia
wantonly lifted her haunches for a no-name greyhound
who came sauntering down from the hillside junkyard.
How's life back home in Minnesota? I hope it's not too bleak."

After you boarded that plane, it rained for two straight weeks.
As the days passed, I began to believe
that I was an umbrella, tasked with sheltering
a wet, dark, hairy creature

who crouched in my rib cage,
complaining incessantly that he was cold, cold, cold.

The Charles River

(Boston, Massachusetts)

REMONSTRANCE

Have you finally cracked? Why would you live some place
you can't see the ocean?
Who could love you if not Poseidon's entourage
of tenderhearts, motherly
mermaids with drenched blue eyes?
What other women could understand
your salt tears? Why
inhabit the Great Plains, a tall and vulnerable
lightning rod? Like a marriage of jellyfish, I know you
are a pair of needy lungs, inflating and deflating with desire.
Here in Massachusetts, brine scents the sky
in a way that masks the small individual
odor of your sex.

THE HARVARD SQUARE STREET MUSICIANS

The Harvard Square street musicians
are short men who look tall
against a background
of cobalt-blue sky;
they tower like pagan heaps of rocks,
intimately tangled
in the grandfatherly
gray beard of sunset.

While the schoolmaster,
fenced in by an erect coalition
of dinner forks,
uses his lips like a pair of shears
to prune the shrubbery
of Hellenistic thought,

the Harvard Square street musicians
soak their goateed chins
in a birdbath of freshly concocted
pizzeria smells
between twanging ballads about the breadlike
tits of local loves.

I always loved this sort of sound—
garage bands when I was a girl—
and now it seems like
I was groomed for this:
my ears patterned their hollowness
after the insides of guitars.

I was betrothed from birth:
I leapt straight
from my swaddling clothes
into this brick pit.

TROUBADOUR'S SONG

Gutless minnow, cast-iron whore,
your eyes are rosy blooms and they are
knives of steel. Your nipples,
my dilapidated virgin, are whalebone
whistles, but also they are keyholes
through which the off-key honey
sloshes out of season. My hunting horn,
my much-worn saddle. The knights in disgrace
ride you through miles of harsh desert
in search of fresh, ferocious game.
They don't want you,
they are sick of kissing your tame thick lips,
your hair which spills upon the dirt
like children's marbles,
your temples that burn like two twin swarms
of fire ants, two sour apples.
Green as the poisoner's cup is your nose,
you are rust skimmed off
the dagger's edge, and your mouth is a nest
full of bird shit, betrayal.

SALISBURY

I clung to your brown jacket like a burr,
my left breast pressed against your tall right flank.
How cold the Massachusetts beaches were.

Only you, whose sinewy grandfather
labored on the tundras, would find this place romantic.
I clung to your brown jacket like a burr,

while your hands plunged deep inside your pockets, where
warmth was. (You'd left your gloves inside the trunk.)
How cold the Massachusetts beaches were,

and how unprepared was I, my eighteen years
clothing me more thinly than a buck-moth's wings.
I clung to your brown jacket like a burr,

to keep myself upright on the sloped earth.
I heard my frozen lips say something cranky.
"How cold the Massachusetts beaches are"

was what I *meant* to say, but how often does
the mouth of youth convey precisely what it thinks?
I clung to your brown jacket like a burr.
How cold, I now say, those Massachusetts beaches were.

LOBSTER

Like a lone old man who grips a cane,
at dusk I spurt out of my sleep
and start to prowl across the plain,

my whiskers tensing when the pulse
of the blue-blooded ocean god
picks up its pace, so each wave rolls

more swiftly past my stony face.
This omen can mean but one thing:
my foe, the codfish, nears these straits,

and I must arm myself for fight.
I was not born to heft a blade;
at birth, my left claw and my right

were equally small, too weak for war.
Chance, or a deity unseen,
then bade me choose my leftmost oar

to train and strengthen, till it grew
to twice the size of my right claw.
With this one gift, I'll now make do.

I'll shape my mouth into a spade
and shovel sand into a song.
I'll heap rocks for a barricade,

and if this battle ends all wrong
and I am reft of every limb,
I'll use my mouth to drag me home.

HAIBUN

At eighteen, I had an overblown fear of losing my virginity.
My subconscious mind transformed this into a phobia of
getting pregnant and having to get an abortion. Two beds
flashed through my mind: first a rumpled dorm room bed
on which we had made love, then a hospital bed with metal
tools laid out at the foot.

It wasn't that he and I didn't want kids together. But we
wanted to wait till we were older. What hubris: believing
we could eat our cake and have it too. Believing we could
abort one child now and have other children later. Believing we could anesthetize our emotions for one afternoon
and reawaken them after. Not realizing that death doesn't
borrow: it only takes.

> Noon sun dries, but cannot heal,
> an umbrella
> the storm turned inside-out

RETURNING TO BOSTON

Like a prepubescent boy dressed in spring leaves,
our bus admired its own reflection in
the River Charles. The river's gray-blue skin
was goosebumped in its short brick-patterned sleeves;

I, too, felt cold and tired, sitting aboard
the bus for hours, watching the uncut
roadside grasses of Connecticut
loll and roll past the tinted window, bored

until now, as my destination city
pulls fully into view, with its arrays
of lit dorm windows in which thin youths raise
their stubbled faces in synchronicity.

Looking back, the two men I loved the most
were the two men who loved Boston the most.

The Hudson River

(New York, New York)

SHADES OF THE LOTUS-EATERS

I am eating your grapes on a concrete roof after nightfall,
watching the Hudson River cold and crinkling
and the distant city lights, which are permanently crinkled
and do not unbend from their brightness.
I'm your beneficiary, the gleaner
of the pleasures you provide. I suck your proffered fruits
one by one off the jutting stems.
I'm a squirrelly scavenger, quick to lay my mouth on any
juice-filled morsel,
any precious minute in which casual charitableness, briefly,
borrows the features of love.

THREE SHORT POEMS ON A COMMON THEME

1.

Staring at you across the room, my body seemed composed
of nothing but eyes.

Even my mouth
watered, like an eye.

2.

I couldn't sleep a wink all night: my brain agitated its solitude
like a washing machine

filled with copies
of your immaculate white shirt.

3.

In the morning, I went out and bought a book of your poems.
It's a poor substitute for a straightedge, it's true,

but you won't
sell me your curves for any price.

THE BORGIAS

Loving you is like eating spaghetti with a spoon:
only the meatball part is easy.
Last night I had that dream again, the one where you are a
       highwayman
who kidnaps me and straps the iron mask over my lower face,
the one that transforms my cries into the clucks of birds,
a hybrid of Alexandre Dumas and H.G. Wells.
"Now anyone who hears you scream
will think you're just a barnyard animal being a barnyard animal,"
       you say.
The barn door slams shut.
I wake up and sit at the kitchen table.
I rub my bare, lipstick-free mouth with my fingertips
and feel giddy. I keep sitting and touching my own lips in awe
till breakfast is done cooking, till the purring toaster
has reached its inevitable climax.

THE CANNIBALS WILL INHERIT THE EARTH

The southern tip of Manhattan is financial:
the city is a mermaid with a golden tail
and theatrical breasts. Or was, until a gale
flung her ashore near a nest of jealous banshees,

who gleefully pinned her down on the beach
and chopped off the lower half of her body.
They left her torso twitching on the bloody
sand, the convexities of her breasts like ostrich

eggs of unappreciated worth exposed
to the sharp air. Crabs crawled up from the sea,
tweaked her teats with their claws. This is where we
enter the tale: we followed the trail of ooze

to where the hemi-corpse lay; and, instead
of grieving what was lost, we feasted on what stayed.

VENETIAN BLINDS

Long-armed sunlight,
yet another tricky fisherwoman,
sifts through her tangle of scarlet-dyed nets
for the little minnow she lost. I'm a different kind of lost:
my heart is an unwieldy bowl of water
that I carry on all my travels
in case I need to dunk my head in brine
and catch my breath when no one's looking.

If I could keep my eyes and windpipe open at the same time,
watching you sleep would be no fatality.
If the needle of my thought didn't falter upon entering
the most delicate of the evening's blue veins.

BOTANICAL GARDEN

I went walking in the botanical garden
till my muscles, like a gashed tree, leaked sour sap.

But the plants beckoned so temptingly,
they tempted me with the promise
that they would tell me their secrets, their secret real names
which not even their pimps know.

Short names, like Chinese peasant girls have:
broom, pink, spurge.

Long names, like disgraced Manhattan socialites:
lacebark pine, threadleaf cypress, littleleaf linden.

Names that made me want to laugh:
beard-tongue, spicebush, sweet box.

Names that made me want to cry:
foamflower, mock orange.

Names that reminded me of high school girlfriends:
bee balm, ladybells, mayapple, meadowsweet.

Names that reminded me of women I once wanted but
        couldn't have:
magic lily, witch hazel, full moon maple.

Names that poked fun at the failings of men:
Adam's needle, Dutchman's breeches, wild sweet William.

Names that glorified the sisterhood of women:
empress tree, motherwort, sweet Cicely.

Your namesake:
impatiens.

My namesake:
inkberry (also known as gallberry).

ART LESSONS

1.

The first lesson is, there is no such thing as a straightedge.
Nor do nude models exist. Should you desire

to produce a straight line, hang a rope
from the ceiling by one end. If, instead, you wish to sketch the human

form, lay a rope along the ground—provided that the ground
is perfectly flat... But one can never be sure of that.

2.

In my dream, your teeth crowded round my tongue, like innocents
come to gawk at a gallows. Then, tired of its orbit, the sun turned

south on a Saturday, singing in a pretty
falsetto down the turnpike

all the way to New Orleans. But it was all for nothing:
my retinas stayed

dark despite all the sun could do, for even the sun knew
a longing too intensely bright

can have no survivors. But tell me: how could you ever
marry that flower girl, the one with the lobster

barrette in her hair? So sweetly her daisies leaned
toward the escaping sun

and cupped the sky in their many
soft white hands, but hands are no excuse.

3.

For the last lesson, take off your jacket,
then all the rest. Lie down on the grass so that

as the sun rises behind you,
I may try and paint your portrait. I suspect

the sun will blind me before I'm through,
but when did eyesight matter? This will be our plan:

if there are no straightedges, we will forge some
out of iron; if there is no nakedness,

we will make some; if there is no sunlight or too much,
the horizon was never a straight line. My dear,

if I'm ever reprieved from hanging, we shall
be lovers. But if I'm ever reprieved from love,

we shall be hangmen, and your silken voice
the rope.

CONFESSIONS

Have you no scruples? Last night, you all but burst
the strings on my guitar,
and this morning I find you swishing your tongue around
in the gap between my piano's pedals,
inciting it to all kinds of ghastly confessions.

I killed your father, it says.
And your mother. And all your ex-lovers, minus one.
I tried to, but his hair just felt so soft
between my fingers...

TANKA (UPPER WEST SIDE)

Winter boy, each of your
fingertips is a bluebird:
I can feel their beaks and
soft cheeks against the inside
of my warm drunk fist.

The Aorta

(Left Ventricle of the Heart)

MARSYAS

Marsyas: was he a faun? a satyr?
From our vantage point, centuries later,
his ethnic background doesn't matter;
what counts is, he was brutally slain.
Vietnamese or Jewish, satyr or faun,
no one lives this kind of horror down.

A gentle outdoors-loving musician,
he was killed in the open, in a Phrygian
forest. With surgical precision,
his murderer peeled his skin off in thin strips
while Marsyas howled through whitened lips.
All day: his howls and the cracks of whips.

Each morning, I show up at my job,
wearing like a fancy watch fob
my stethoscope. At times, I want to drop
the old thing on the ground and sputter,
"Apollo, patron god of doctors,
deity to whom we pray, 'Save us from slaughter,

protect us from disease'! How could you
be he to whom we pray for tidings good, you
who tortured Marsyas in the Phrygian wood?
How could you cause such suffering?
And what's your planned penitential offering?
Remorse is nothing; sunbeams are nothing."

CAESAREAN SECTION

The top of Baby's head was tinged with blue,
like a wad of foreign money. Greedily,
the doctor yanked, and upward Baby flew.

Mother's skin was a friendly cottony hue;
her uterus was pink as reverie.
But the top of Baby's head was tinged with blue.

If a vegetable of that color grew
in a field, I wouldn't touch it; I'd leave it be.
But the doctor yanked, and upward Baby flew.

Once Baby had surfaced and lay in plain view,
we saw he was as whole as you or me,
though the top of his head was tinged with blue.

"A healthy infant," the stern nurse approved.
Eyes glazed like caramel corn, Mom sighed happily.
With Baby in her arms, the nurse then flew

over to the other side of the small room,
where she jotted Baby's data on a sheet.
By then, Baby's flesh no longer looked blue.
Up from his flabby mouth, a cross cry flew.

ELEGY

Of the poor folk who lie moaning in their hospital beds,
Dr. Robbins had only this to say:
"Their intestinal parasites have no bones
and therefore are rarely detected by X-rays."

But what killed the old Nepalese woman wasn't
the 10-inch worm that burrowed in her gut,
wallowing in her smells. It was something less orderly,
less sequential, more cloudlike: metastatic breast cancer.

Good sir, no matter how straight your posture at the boardroom table,
your intestines are as convoluted as hers.
I wonder: when she died, did her tapeworm outlive her
by a minute, or two, or several? And did it feel a sense of loss?

CHARCOAL DRAWING OF DR. CLARIBEL CONE

Claribel Cone:
today her name's unknown
outside of Baltimore.
She was one of thirteen heirs
of a fertile Jewish pair
who owned a grocery store.

Cone never took a spouse,
but shared a Maryland house
with her sister till she died.
One of few ambitious ladies
who in the 1880s
went to medical school, she tried

for as long as she lived
"to be approved of
as woman and as worker"
by her male peers.
Then, in her fortieth year,
Cone was distracted from this endeavor

by her meeting with "the Beast
(*le Fauve*)," Henri Matisse.
Funny that Cone, who wore
a bow tie at her chin
and concealed her fat legs in
black skirts that brushed the floor,

patronized this painter of nudes,
of odalisques who exude
servility toward men.
Matisse described his art
in this way once: "It starts
as flirtation, but it ends

as rape; it ravishes me."
Did Cone secretly thrill to see
his violently colored shapes?
What furtive feelings beset her,
causing her to turn abettor
in his grandiose Jovian rapes?

THE PICKLED WOMB

In a shallow tub,
my assistants brought me
the chopped-up heart
of the bitter vegetable
called woman. The jigsaw
pieces of the thing
had been embalmed
in formaldehyde
till they were firm and impassive
as automotive rubber—
these chunky fragments
that once had comprised
the core of a volatile,
sensitive girl.
As with Humpty Dumpty,
the white and the yellow
were so mutilated, they
couldn't be distinguished.
Like the first air-breathing lungfish
to slither onto dry dirt,
all that seems barbaric
and backward to us was
once the state of the art.

TANKA (EPITAPH FOR A YOUNG WOMAN)

Her love for her husband
was like saffron,
a spice made by grinding
a crocus's female sex organs
till just powder remains.

The River Styx

(Hades)

ADA LOVELACE

(1815-1852)

1.

My father named me Augusta,
and my mother permitted the naming.

Why did she permit it,
knowing our family secrets?
If words can be sinful,
names are very hellfire.

I think my father felt ashamed of his sin,
the sin he'd committed together with my aunt Augusta.
He never called me by my Christian name
but nicknamed me Ada.

2.

I barely knew my father. He left
before I learned how to speak, name things, ask questions.

When I learned how to speak, I said,
"My head hurts."
And: "I can't move my legs."
And: "Sometimes my eyes go blind."

Doctors came to our house and prodded me
with their steel instruments, their pork-red hands.
Mother knew many doctors; she sat downstairs
sipping tea with them for hours.

The doctors soothed Mother's fears. She said,
"Well, better an illness of the body than of the mind."

3.

One of Mother's most trusted confidants
was a hobbling, grandfatherly man. "This, Ada, is Mr. Friend.
I have asked him to tutor you in mathematics.
Mathematics, Ada, refreshes and strengthens the mind."

I felt at ease with Mr. Friend. Like the doctors,
he seemed not to notice the breasts
that, when I was ten,
sprouted beneath my dress like one-eyed potatoes.

Mr. Friend talked to me about algebra as if I were a boy.
He seized up geometric concepts as though they were cold-blooded eels,
sliced off their heads, and proceeded
to dissect them with sexless fervor.

"So what if you're a girl?" he wheezed.
"Why shouldn't a girl study mathematics?"

Then, one day, the eels came alive for me,
and I felt as if I were standing on their backs,
and they were helping me walk on water.

4.

From then on, my mind was a fully functioning piano,
unlike other girls' brains, clogged with the soft mush of poetry.
I began to feel sure of myself,
sure of Mother's unspoken approval.

Then, one night, I met Father's colleague
Mr. Hobhouse at a party. I sneered at him
as Mother had taught me to do, but he wasn't scared away.
Poetically, he stroked his dyed mustache.

"Young lady," he mused,
"your mouth is exactly like Lord Byron's."

CARO

(1785-1828)

I am no longer your lover, but I shall ever remember with gratitude the many instances I have received of the predilection you have shewn in my favour. I shall ever continue your friend, if your Ladyship will permit me so to style myself; and, as a first proof of my regard, I offer you this advice: correct your vanity, which is ridiculous; exert your absurd caprices upon others; and leave me in peace.
—Lord Byron, in a letter to Lady Caroline Lamb, November 1812

Carrow: an Irish word, signifying a gambler.
My cousin Caroline, nicknamed "Caro,"
with spaniel-like blonde curls,
her rib cage frail and diminutive,
her breasts massless and witchily perfumed
as white trumpet flowers: *she* was no Irishwoman,
though she spent considerable time in that country
"for the sake of her health," not least in 1813
when trying to recover from a brain malady
the scandal rags termed "erotomania."
What this "erotomania" *was*, no two doctors could agree on.
Said one London specialist: "Perhaps no brain malady at all
but an illness of the womb, an intemperate dampness,
an unseasonable heat, unbecoming in a peeress nearly thirty
years old, the wife of a cuckolded statesman too timid
to whip her into good behavior." Her paramour, a clubfooted
poet fond of the Greek style of love and famed
for vulgar verses, soon tired of the fiery
Caro; she clung like morning glory.
She tracked him like a bloodhound, wagering
she could win back his love through fanciful ploys:
one time, to the disgrace of us all,
she disguised herself as a high-voiced servant-boy
to penetrate his bedroom. Another time, she mailed
him an effusive love letter, enclosing (I blush to say it)

66

a beribboned lock of her own pubic hair
as a token of her esteem. He fled to Greece to escape her;
poor Caro, in sorrow, got drunk on spirits and laudanum and died.
Now, whatever clergymen may mutter
about the "modern generation," we may at least say *this* in its defense:
unlike the old-fashioned Caro, addicted to eros,
modern girls would never gamble away their very
life for love.

SAPPHO

(630 B.C.??? - 570 B.C.???)

Phaon, my faithless lover,
have no doubt about it:
when we are both dead
and summoned before the tribunal of Hades,
he is bound to uphold
my righteous claim
and punish you
for your waywardness.
He will take my side
because he loves me.
Hell's habitants all love me
because I sing them my best songs.
And, unlike the pragmatic Orpheus,
who only sang to them when he needed their help
to resuscitate his bride,
I sing to Hell's habitants year-round
and never stoop to ask them to play
the role of procuress.

BAD BLOOD

When you, like me, are dead and underground,
my ghost will hasten to Hades's anteroom
so that I can be first to kiss your brow
and welcome you to hell, our new shared home.

I'll kiss you, tastefully and not too loud,
in the presence of Hades's pollen-dusted wife,
and clutch your trembling hand, which was too proud
to cling to mine while you were still alive.

"You thought you could escape me, Phaon?" I'll tease,
"You thought you could replace me with young girls,
awkward Sicilians who don't know their knees
from their noses, but who have long blonde curls?
You thought you could get rid of me, who sweat
full-formed iambics and am always wet?"

LULLABY

You, out of all of us, are least in need
of being lullabied:
you, Miró's bronze lightning-bird,
you, the saint with the teardrop head.

The hound of song has cornered you, up high
in a leafless, fruitless tree.
You sing your own hot lullaby;
its wax-drops drip all night on me.

You, out of all of us, are least in need
of being crooned to sleep.
I've seen you smile while no one peeped:
two rows of noon-hot, naked teeth.

I've seen you smile, and not a girl in town
can attest she's seen you weep.
What use is lullabying, then?
What use is it to such strong men?

Last night, I dreamed I saw you sitting proud
at a table on a cloud.
Then, from a jug with a tooth-marked spout,
I saw you slake your ulcered mouth.

I watched you drink the way a dolphin would;
your face was blue and cold.
And when your appetite was spoiled,
you gobbled pills embossed with mold.

What can we dreamers of the world give you
besides our lullaby?
You, Miró's bronze lightning-bird;
you, the saint with the teardrop head.

THE BEEKEEPER'S MASK

Some mortal women have taken me to task
because I jilted the god with wasp-gold wings,
preferring you, who have a sharper sting.
They wish I did not wear the beekeeper's mask
with such airs, I suppose. Last night, newly gored,
I bathed for pleasure in the salty sea
as though the brine in my wounds brought joy to me;
and heard those ladies mutter, spitting on the water,
"She's only a goddess, but fancies she's a whore.
She flaunts the blindfold he makes her wear in bed,
as though it takes a genius to play the fool."
Spit floats; blood sinks to the bottom of the pool.

VILLANELLE FOR LOUISE BOURGEOIS (1911-2010)

I was a runaway girl who turned out alright.
—Louise Bourgeois

I was a runaway girl who turned out alright.
All the algebraists who hump the pillars of the Sorbonne
couldn't stop me from running nude into the New York City night.

The tapestries of centuries past, their unicorns and wights,
couldn't trip up my running shoes: I could not choose but run.
I was a runaway girl who turned out alright.

My father mended rugs for money; he ate my nanny's rug for spite.
To flee the prick of his unicorn horn, I married young:
with my bridegroom, I fled nude into the New York City night.

If I'd had to, I would've gladly made a solo flight
à la Amelia Earhart; I'm used to doing things alone.
I was a runaway girl who turned out alright—

Look at me now, surrounded by Manhattan's neon lights!
What a palace this place is! Who truly needs the sun
when they're running nude in the blue New York City night?

Never mind how lonely I get amid these steel-girt heights,
or the guilt I feel when I recall the war-torn France I shunned.
I was a runaway girl who turned out alright,
running, running nude into the New York City night.

HYMN TO APHRODITE

You who are prouder of your affectionate nature than anything,
you whose bright eyes
remind me of two sovereigns who wear
their luminous wedding-rings outside their gloves,

teach me to stop hiding gems
between the woolen and my skin.

Teach me to stop trying to mix
shyness and love,
two substances that are as averse to mixing as
oil and tears.

VESPERS

Like tongues dyed green
by lime candy-flakes,
the backyard lizards
and the backyard snakes
roll from side to side
in the tight-lipped dark.

Their bodies are as liquid
as snowmelt in the spring.
Their bodies are enormous,
or so one would think
from the loudness of
the hissing sounds they make.

It's a deafening noise,
like the din of a god
who smacks his deathless lips,
watching women sunbathe nude
on the decks of tiny ships
on the Dead Sea puttering.

Or the clamor a camera makes
rapid-fire, monotone,
as the cameraman lurks
in the trees outside the pad
of a scantily-clad
young girl who lives alone.

THE DAY BEFORE ALL THE NAMES CHANGED

The two ladies' names tattooed on my uncle's forearm
read in opposite directions
now, but tomorrow both
will flow toward magnetic north.

If you're planning to get married,
it's best to do it tonight
before the names all change
and you no longer know whose bloodline
you're getting tangled with.

Constantine the Accursed,
you have the same surname as me
already, so we may as well
marry each other. Meet me at the church
of Saint Cecilia at dusk.

Don't be discouraged if the church
no longer goes by that name
by the time you arrive. It's a sandstone building with blue
marble wings. And I'll be the only bride
wearing carnations, loops of blood-red
carnations, and nothing else.

About the Author

Jenna Le is a second-generation Vietnamese-American, born and raised just outside Minneapolis, Minnesota. She holds degrees from Harvard University (a B.A. in Mathematics) and Columbia University (an M.D.).

About NYQ Books™

NYQ Books™ was established in 2009 as an imprint of The New York Quarterly Foundation, Inc. Its mission is to augment the *New York Quarterly* poetry magazine by providing an additional venue for poets already published in the magazine. A lifelong dream of NYQ's founding editor, William Packard, NYQ Books™ has been made possible by both growing foundation support and new technology that was not available during William Packard's lifetime. We are proud to present these books to you and hope that you will continue to support The New York Quarterly Foundation, Inc. and our poets and that you will enjoy these other titles from NYQ Books™:

Barbara Blatner	*The Still Position*
Amanda J. Bradley	*Hints and Allegations*
rd coleman	*beach tracks*
Joanna Crispi	*Soldier in the Grass*
Ira Joe Fisher	*Songs from an Earlier Century*
Sanford Fraser	*Tourist*
Tony Gloeggler	*The Last Lie*
Ted Jonathan	*Bones & Jokes*
Richard Kostelanetz	*Recircuits*
Iris Lee	*Urban Bird Life*
Linda Lerner	*Takes Guts and Years Sometimes*
Gordon Massman	*0.174*
Michael Montlack	*Cool Limbo*
Kevin Pilkington	*In the Eyes of a Dog*
Jim Reese	*ghost on 3rd*
F. D. Reeve	*The Puzzle Master and Other Poems*
Jackie Sheeler	*Earthquake Came to Harlem*
Jayne Lyn Stahl	*Riding with Destiny*
Shelley Stenhouse	*Impunity*
Tim Suermondt	*Just Beautiful*
Douglas Treem	*Everything so Seriously*
Oren Wagner	*Voluptuous Gloom*
Joe Weil	*The Plumber's Apprentice*
Pui Ying Wong	*Yellow Plum Season*
Fred Yannantuono	*A Boilermaker for the Lady*
Grace Zabriskie	*Poems*

Please visit our website for these and other titles:

www.nyqbooks.org

CPSIA information can be obtained
at www.ICGtesting.com
Printed in the USA
LVOW11s0351040117
519673LV00001B/149/P

UNMANLY GRIEF

Miller Williams Poetry Series
EDITED BY BILLY COLLINS

UNMANLY GRIEF

POEMS BY

JESS WILLIARD

The University of Arkansas Press
Fayetteville
2019

ISBN: 978-1-68226-093-7
eISBN: 978-1-61075-662-4

23 22 21 20 19   5 4 3 2 1

Designed by Liz Lester

♾ The paper used in this publication meets the minimum requirements
of the American National Standard for Permanence of Paper for Printed
Library Materials Z39.48-1984.

Library of Congress Cataloging-in-Publication Data

Names: Williard, Jess, 1991–   author.
Title: Unmanly grief / poems by Jess Williard.
Description: Fayetteville : The University of Arkansas Press, 2019. | Series:
  Miller Williams poetry series
Identifiers: LCCN 2018037837 | ISBN 9781682260937 (pbk. : alk. paper)
Classification: LCC PS3623.I5744 A6 2019 | DDC 811/.6--dc23
LC record available at https://lccn.loc.gov/2018037837

Funded in part by

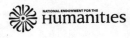

MILLER AND LUCINDA WILLIAMS
POETRY FUND

For my dad

CONTENTS

THREE

■ ■ ■

SERIES EDITOR'S PREFACE

When the University of Arkansas Press invited me to be the editor of its annual publication prize named in honor of Miller Williams—the longtime director of the press and its poetry program—I was quick to accept. Since 1988, when he published my first full-length book, *The Apple that Astonished Paris*, I have felt keenly indebted to Miller. Among the improvements to the world made by Miller before his death in January 2015 at the age of eighty-four was his dedication to publishing a poet's first book every year. He truly enjoyed finding a place for new poets on the literary stage. In 1990, this commitment became official when the first Arkansas Poetry Prize was awarded. Fittingly, upon his retirement, the prize was renamed the Miller Williams Poetry Prize.

When Miller first spotted my poetry, I was forty-six years old with only two chapbooks to my name. Not a pretty sight. Miller was the one who carried me across that critical line, where the "unpublished poets" impatiently wait, and who made me, in one stroke, a "published poet." Funny, you never hear "unpublished novelist." I suppose if you were a novelist who remained unpublished you would stop writing novels. Not the case with many poets, including me.

Miller Williams was more than my first editor. Over the years, he and I became friends, but even more importantly, before I knew him, I knew his poems. His straightforward, sometimes folksy, sometimes witty, and always trenchant poems were to me models of how poems might sound and how they could *go*. He was one of the poets who showed me that humor had a legitimate place in poetry—that a poem could be humorous without being silly or merely comical. He also showed me that a plain-spoken poem did not have to be imaginatively plain or short on surprises. He was one of my literary fathers.

Miller occupied a solid position on the American literary map, though considering his extensive career and steady poetic output, it's surprising that his poems don't enjoy even more prominence. As his daughter became the well-known singer and recording artist that she is today, Miller came to be known as the father of Lucinda Williams. Miller and Lucinda even appeared on stage together several times, performing a father-daughter act of song and poetry. In 1997, Miller came to the nation's attention when Bill Clinton chose him to be the inaugural poet at his second inauguration. The poem he wrote for that day, "Of History and Hope," is a meditation on how "we have memorized America." In turning to the children of our country, he broadens a nursery rhyme question by asking "How does *our* garden grow?" Miller knew that occasional poems, especially for occasions of such importance, are notoriously difficult—some would say impossible—to write with success. But he rose to that occasion and produced a winner. His confident reading of the poem before the nation added cultural and emotional weight to the morning's ceremony and lifted Miller Williams to a new level of popularity and respect.

Miller was pleased by public recognition. What poet is immune? At home one evening, spotting a headline in a newspaper that read POET BURNS TO BE HONORED, Miller's wife Jordan remarked "They sure have your number." Of course, it was the day dedicated annually to honoring Robert Burns.

Miller's true legacy lies in his teaching and his career as a poet, which covered four decades. In that time, he produced over a dozen books of his own poetry and literary theory. His poetic voice tends to be soft-spoken but can be humorous or bitingly mordant. The poems sound like speech running to a meter. And they show a courteous, engaging awareness of the presence of a reader. Miller knew that the idea behind a good poem is to make the reader feel something, rather than to merely display the poet's emotional state, which has a habit of boiling down to one of the many forms of misery. Miller also possessed the authority of experience to produce poems that were just plain wise.

With Miller's sensibility in mind, I set out to judge the first year's contest. I was on the lookout for poems that resembled Miller's. But the more I read, the more I realized that applying such narrow criteria would be selling Miller short and not being fair to the entrants. It would make more sense to select manuscripts that Miller would enjoy reading for their own merits, not for their similarity to his own poems. That his tastes in poetry were broader than the territory of his own verse can be seen in the variety of the books he published. The list included poets as different from one another as John Ciardi and Jimmy Carter. Broadening my own field of judgment brought happy results, and I'm confident that Miller would enthusiastically approve of this year's selections, as well as those in previous years.

This year, the work of two very different poets, who have readability, freshness of language, and seriousness of intent in common, stood out from the tall stack of submissions. Miller would be pleased to know that, as it turned out, this will be a first book for the both of the two winners, born thirty-five years apart.

■ ■ ■

Jess Williard's poems often begin with the kind of narrative information we are used to getting in a short story. One opens "Jordy paid me seventeen dollars and two peach/ White Owls to box his cousin in a clearing." (That "peach" deserves its special position.) And "Townie Elegy" reminded me of Updike's short story "A&P." The poems in *Unmanly Grief* are American in the way that famous Updike story is. They take place typically in the teen world of baseball, wrestling, and bagging groceries. Some readers may be made to feel right at home, but along with this slightly cozy familiarity comes a series of maneuvers and images that assure us we are in the hands of an adept poet. "Lean deeper down between/ the seats and it's 1994" reminds us of the flexibility of time in poetry. Lines like "An infant swaddled/ in a Motel 6 dresser drawer" show the indelibility of certain images we encounter in poems. And here, the verbal stops us in our tracks: ". . . the push/pull full body lift split I'd adopted from a thick farmer/ named Kevin." We recognize that Williard typically uses a narrative to disguise his subtler intentions and the deeper, wider implications of his subjects.

Kevin, by the way, is not the only guy in these poems. There's Clif, an adopted child, Jordy of the White Owl, and "dad" who lets his son take him down in wrestling every time. The reappearance of some of these figures adds to the sense that we have been brought into a community of people and influences that is—or more likely was—the poet's daily world.

Whether Williard favors couplets or meatier single-stanza poems, he knows how to break a line and how to replicate the rhythms of natural speech. His are natural-sounding poems that lead us to striking insights and strange destinations. The most clearly felt aspect of these poems has to do with the poet always being *present*, available to the reader, and never using language as a hedge to hide behind. The last lines of "Soundstripe," a poem which oddly integrates music into wrestling, gives us a model of the poet's arrival and simultaneous wanting for more: "This is the set up: the train pulls into the station/ I step out and look for the stairs."

Billy Collins

ACKNOWLEDGMENTS

Grateful acknowledgment to the following publications in which poems from this manuscript first appeared, sometimes in earlier versions: *The American Journal of Poetry*: "Even," "Shadowbox," and "Watch For It Everywhere"; *Adirondack Review*: "For Floyd Patterson: A Letter"; *Barrow Street*: "A Man in the Stands," and "Heat"; *Borderlands: Texas Poetry Review*: "Filament"; *Cider Press Review*: "Practice"; *Cold Mountain Review*: "Feat"; *Connotation Press*: "Doctrines on Getting Lost"; *Cumberland River Review*: "To Clarey"; *CURA: A Literary Magazine of Art & Action*: "Worth It"; *december*: "Following"; *Electric Literature*: "At McKinley Aquatics Center," and "Generous"; *Fogged Clarity*: "Townie Elegy"; *Grist*: "On Boxing," and "Rod"; *The Hampden-Sydney Poetry Review*: "Float"; *Iron Horse Literary Review*: "Siren for Manny Pacquiao"; *Kestrel*: "Grace to Our Spines"; *The McNeese Review*: "Apologia"; *The New Orleans Review*: "Andronicus with Tar"; *Ninth Letter*: "The Spoils"; *Poet Lore*: "Look"; *Oxford Poetry*: "The Problem of Ankles"; *Passages North:* "Collateral"; *Ruminate Magazine*: "Soundstripe"; *Silk Road Review*: "Hands"; *Southern Humanities Review*: "Most High"; *Superstition Review*: "The Touching"; *Wisconsin People & Ideas*: "Let's Intuit Something."

"Feat" was an Honorable Mention for the 2018 R.T. Smith Prize for narrative poetry from Cold Mountain Review.

"Soundstripe" was a finalist for the 2016 Janet B. McCabe prize in poetry from Ruminate Magazine.

Immense thanks to Billy Collins for his careful and compassionate eye, and to Molly Bess Rector, Melissa Ann King, David Scott Cunningham, and everyone else at the University of Arkansas Press. For their early (crucial) guidance and continued support I'd like to thank Ryan Black, Nicole Cooley, and the Queens College English department. My spirit continues to be bolstered by my mentors at the University of Illinois at

Urbana-Champaign: Mike Madonick, Brigit Kelly, Janice Harrington, Jodee Stanley, and Steve Davenport. I am eternally grateful. Thanks to Beth Gylys for the relentless encouragement. Boundless love and gratitude to my writing comrades, without whom this book would not exist, and who are also the greatest friends: Mike Hurley, John Dudek, Zach McVicker, Sara Fan, Matt Minicucci, Taylor Micks, and Skyler Lalone. Thank you, finally and most fundamentally, to my brother, my sister, my mom, and my dad.

A Man in the Stands

Because a boy named Clif was taken below
the away team bleachers and beaten
by a stranger in a trench coat, there's a game
the boys play where they push
one another into the darkened hovel
and box each other's ears till they are dizzy,
then run. I can hear the muffs and open-
palmed punches between laughs
and pleading shrieks. I can feel the trellised
benches shake, can almost reach through,
grab the collars and say
Enough. He's had enough. To reach
through is to reach back,
and it's 2003. Lean deeper down between
the seats and it's 1994. Actually grasp
at one of their shoulders and it's 1989
where Clif is waiting in a badly lit pediatric
unit to be adopted, his parents four states
away strangling the classifieds
in a week-old newspaper. The call,
the five-hour drive. An infant swaddled
in a Motel 6 dresser drawer. The summer
stars wet and brilliant above. But before
he's taken home, a nurse comes
to his crying, cradles his head and traces
each of his small ears with her thumb. *Enough.*
That's enough. Eased into silence, he sleeps.
Someone gropes blindly through the ceiling.

ONE

On Boxing

On borrowing your sister's foundation, any of the shudders her body
releases when she fails at holding your face as she weeps.

On Floyd Patterson and the kisses he'd place on the foreheads
of the men he knocked out, how he'd pull them up, slumped

in their corners, to make the eight-count and just hug them for a while.
On being driven home from the tournament through slumbering

summer dusk. Fields swept at a speed into song. Someone whistles
how heart is heart and has little to do with the thickness of your neck.

Because you are a slight boy, bent to bring home no violence.
On slightness, though it cannot carry much. On bearing, or how

to handle men when to hurt them was never the point. On where to tilt
the bulb so the bruises turn to shadows.

Practice

And this shaft of barn door light, the dirt and rock strip
between our blue house and someone else's matted lawn,

a tired web of orange-powdered wire in between, and this breath
of upset dust, and my brother, gravel spraying from his heels,

rocks clinging to his wake like so many hovering dust motes.
We're racing. But regardless of who's always the faster one

and regardless of where, if at all, this stratifies us, and on what list,
he's not waiting this time. It's only for me that this exists

in stasis—I'm so far behind that I'm pumping now for the privilege
of catching some of the dust he kicks back between the cracks

of my teeth and cursing when I blow soot and blood clots
onto my pillowcase in the morning. If I'm lucky, a rock

he's sent flying will clip one of my canines and I'll tongue a silver tooth
like the one Jordy wears at football practices and takes out

when he's on dates with nice girls. This is all completely still for me
and I can breathe in it. And this alphabetical anchor of the track team,

left to race alone each week at the end of each meet, and each time
I make a new still world, whether it's gravel levitating at his back

or scraps of chewed tire. In each I'm working to breathe
debris, digging in my toes to make his wreckage inhabit me.

The Problem of Ankles

If you think of the song as data, my sister is missing.

In the street, the chair-bound Hmong father prods his spokes
to a steady climb. Street ruts play around his children playing,
around the tubes of his wheels in almost-alive avoidance.

Sometimes I get glimpses of his legs: in this late June courting
sourly humid afternoons he wears shorts.
Shins like quarter notes. No calves.

And dusk, riding home, his kids bouncing balls to summon
bats from streetlamp posts—two white shafts
skirting peaceably against what I'd imagine possible.

And my sister?
Tuning a transistor to mark her next move?
Calling to request that same song on every FM station?

Try the AM and a nonmedical but professional opinion
suggests that Lonnie Ballentine is a prototypical NFL

defensive back, that he certainly looks the part. *Skinny ankles*,
the scouting report offers. This before anything else.

And when, between plays of his professional debut,
Lonnie salutes a boy in the stands wearing his jersey,
what other conjunction than between a leg and a foot?

Because the most my mother can do now is send a phantom
to worry about the storms where her daughter might be,

one of three places in separate time zones
where it'd be a privilege to scowl at the horizon,
to cower at a descending wall of hail

that's sure to ride out the low-pressure system into the rest
of the plains, what might be a country or a ribcage
or a spare bedroom decked out for no one, no baby.

But here's a baby, two knots of cartilage in the storm
of a sonogram: ankles.

She'll come out that way, the doctor says,
miming a pull with his hands wrapped
around two small, invisible feet.

We'll see first the parts that carry the rest away.

For Floyd Patterson: A Letter

It starts with my father curled on the floor
at the foot of his granddaughter's bed,

      don't leave uttered for a second,
        then third time, enough not to shake

the strange urgency of her three-year-old
imperative,

      this the third night my sister
      hasn't shown up—

don't leave. He will sleep
but not dream. He will wake

      to a world that asks him to teach
      a language to people who could not possibly

hear it. The man has never been large.
And here, cradling dank air

      so a three-year-old body lax atop cotton bedding
      may measure a kind of closeness:

the man has never been large.
I do not need to mention the boxer,

all that humming, side-bending sinew,
unrelentingly tender even inside

a ring, his curled body at the foot of anything;
compactness, his compactness, his compactness—

I do not need to mention him silently
dismantling everything.

The man has never been large.
And any history where two men

circle each other with intention
is a packaged history where one

will stop and lay on the ground
to quell the other's loneliness. There is purpose

here. There is something to send
from a cower. It starts where it shouldn't

and becomes mention of this world
where to be small and furious is enough.

Townie Elegy

If I told you bagging groceries to pay for community college tuition
and a gym membership made me feel some kind of glamorous
it would be mostly honest and mostly, as I was then, ignorant
of any real responsibility outside of anthropology text books
and the push/pull full-body lift split I'd adopted from a thick farmer
named Kevin. It was the work, though, and that I owned
what I was learning and what I was filling beneath my skin
that made hating what I didn't know about myself something crucial
to wake up to and knead. If you've grown up in a college
town, let's say this together: I'm not from a nice place.
On the fringes of academic enclaves are the battered and battering.
If it's romantic or autumnal for waves of men to make trips
to campus drinking wells, to coax dizzy nineteen-year-olds
into their truck cabs, then it's also important to pause
before reminding me that these things happen everywhere—
They don't. Not like this. Measured against the beautiful-
brained and impermanent, how can we not be a little grotesque?
What if I told you that although he pointed to the stud in my ear
and called me *sweet heart, fairy heart*, the father of a friend received
my rapt attention because he once worked masonry on St. Patrick's
Cathedral? That the job trumped the man? How ridiculous
I must have sounded asking questions about New York City.
How full of sputtering nothing. But the grocery store made way
for all the other necessary industries. Gym memberships
cost about the same anywhere. And though I never did go hunting

with him, I believed Kevin when he told me that to rise at three
and sit in the stock-still air of a tree stand made killing *more or less*
a ritual of waking up. He made four thousand dollars selling venison
and racks that season. Enough for another two semesters tuition.
So holler at me, he told me, *if you more or less need something to do.*

Doctrines on Getting Lost

What could have been believed: the Quaker meeting house
and other shuttered rituals, God actually moving people

to speak in a room full of bowed heads. But I played baseball
and the parasol of the soft-toss was infinitely more to lay faith in

than something like a library for ambivalent believers.
It was here, in the sodden boiler room of a prewar clinic,

where I got lost for the first time. There were lights in my shoes
and you could follow me in a laser vigil. Believe in that.

Believe in no crust and the way bats dive for tossed bits of gravel
as if they were insects, as if there weren't really a driveway

or lies being thrown straight up into the sky. Believe in this:
my parents—gorgeous, stooping people who have probably loved

too much—adopted two infants from rural New Jersey and married
without telling anyone. Believe in the crosscut and blister bulge

of lawn-mowing and running for no reason, running for miles.
But you believed in the miles. The second and not the last time

I was lost it was because I drank before I knew how with older,
heavier boys, and woke on the sooty beach of Lake Monona.

Water lapped at my heels and the soft tide sounded like an exhale,
like something older and more tired than human saying, *Hal-le, Lu-jah.*

Rod

Jordy paid me seventeen dollars and two peach
White Owls to box his cousin in a clearing
where you could see, if you craned,
the cursing lights of cars on his overpass.
His because its where he painted, smoked, and I think
sometimes slept. The mosquitos were crazy that year—
plump, whiskered things—and I was moving fast
if only to slip sick neck tickles in the night-wet air,
moving too because Jordy thought it'd be funny
to give Raul regular sparring gloves
and for me to wear some Incredible Hulk Gamma
Green Smash Fists he'd found in his basement,
                          moving to parry
plodding jabs with these veined foam fists
that yelled in the superhero's comically
guttural voice if you smacked them hard enough
together or against something else.
It only took five punches for the plastic handle
inside the left one to snap, tear through the foam
and rake a glistening track into Raul's cheek.
I'm the one calling it, Jordy said, *and I have not
called it.*
              The mosquitos were crazy
that year and curtailed an otherwise drawn-out
summer, cut nights short when training outside
became unbearable. So we trained inside instead
and came out in September a company of lean,

pale apostles. The ground was beginning to cool.
We used the word *shook* in every sentence.
Why are you acting so shook? We had them shook,
man. Believe I wasn't shook, though. That night
Jordy and I walked the cutback trail to the clearing
where he kicked the dirt around in a few places,
dropped into a squat and double-handed dig,
excavated the jagged plastic handle and walked
towards me, holding it like a divining rod.

Filament

Tungsten, no—
the sciatica a flicker of some other wire buoyed in flesh.
The fire that ignited down the backs of his legs
when his head met the pavement emitted no light,
but you could feel the heat if you held a hand
within a few inches of his back. For a year he floated
whenever he thought he was walking. Spine:
uncapped flare held to the sky then placed
in increments along a bend in the highway.
Anyone can be alerted to their own wreck,
their pathways, their twining bush of nerves.
Of course it was about a girl, before he knew
he could keep something he wasn't hurting
himself for, before he cursed, tripped backward
over a book bag, figured what to call this incidental
glowing.

Andronicus with Tar

To drop the end of a roofing hatchet
on Stone Coat single shear, to watch it slap

and flail from the ripped slate,
is not to say that a dying woman

kissed me on the mouth on a visit
to Mercy Manor North. That's not part

of the conversation. Roof-work testimony
needs conquest, and this I owe our driftless

shift crew. A carburetor is dashing air
against fuel to push these nails

through condo joists, so I will try
and give: she pulled down her respirator

and beckoned in for a secret. I was fourteen.
Air through her bristled nostrils spoke

corporeal, aspirated in a pleasant lisp
the word *assailants*. I imagined that, though—

I heard the word through the exhale.
Haven't figured out what to do

with knowing it. I do know that when Titus
asks his mute daughter to speak she will try,

though she has no tongue. She will pinch
a twig between the stumps of her arms

and etch the names of her attackers in peat.
Bent to scrawl *Aaron, Demetrius, Chiron,*

maybe, into the worked-in acid dirt.
To kneel and expose. Formal nouns

will stack their spines on any ground.
And unless this work is violent

or the inscription of a phantom limb
is illegible, the wrist curl

with curved blade to separate tar
and rock sheet is a quiet gesture.

I will return home and move away,
taking with me from the roofs little more

than callused hands. Little more
than a name.

For Claudius

For Claudius, *sweet and commendable* is a compliment given
in order to control; Hamlet's grief must be lightened for a semblance
of ease in the new kingship. The nation wants a happy royal
family. Hamlet must know what's lost is finally lost—
ghosts are unconvincing. For five acts he wades dumbfounded
through the low pools of mourning. But this is the part
I lost out on. What I got from that cold script
read was Menelaus. Rasmussen Women's Theater
was doing a rendition of *Helen*, and I had shoulder-length hair
and could grow a beard. Looked about right for the part.
Menelaus is a man lost, but not like Hamlet. His phantom
is his wife. In this version she never makes it to Troy,
instead spends seventeen years in an Egyptian hotel room.
They reunite, of course, but it's different then. The woman
cast opposite me as the exiled queen was a decade older.
She knew the landscapes of childbirth and divorce,
the bodies of men she'd read and then forgotten, and I longed
for her the way boys long for things, though my license
to that sanction had already expired. We practiced lines
in the backs of libraries on the kinds of autumn evenings
that make the sky seem like it's sighing. Sometimes I held
her infant son. I was poor for the part: my voice octaves above
where a soldier's should be, I showed an embarrassing
earnestness in monologues about death, the ravages of time
and war. The director told me once to stop floating
when I spoke.

       So I did. And because Helen's projection

is cast by gods to divert the king, Menelaus is protecting
an apparition. To move on is a difficult thing. *To persevere in obstinate
condolement*, says Claudius, *is a course of impious stubbornness*.
Menelaus keeps looking. Hamlet, too, but what he finds is not
what it's about. This is what it's about: the woman
who sat in the front row on opening night, the way
she kept tucking her bangs behind her ears. Or the man
who took my hands in his in the lobby afterwards,
stared directly into my face and assured me I'd eventually
be *believable as a hero*; that if I kept working I could *assume
the leading man*. That my voice would deepen. It didn't.
'Tis unmanly grief to dwell so indulgently. *It shows a will
most incorrect to heaven*. This is all to get Hamlet
to let go. And whether it's an act of conscience or simply
an act, it is Claudius attempting to put something to rest.
The actor who won that role was so wrong for the part.
Too sure of himself to pretend. Too much of a man.

Kissing At

When it was a yard it was filled with curious brambles,
scrambling things.
Holes for animals wide like yawns
and the tough smell of rusted metal.

Ferns crept from the dew-dank musk
of the forgotten garage basement
where the soft soot of sunlessness
bred white things, white like covered grass.
They had no eyes.

When it was a workshop, Jordy welded things.
It was boring work to watch,
the way bugs on pins in frames are boring.
Afterwards we would take a ride to nowhere in particular,
in the Nova or the Galaxie,
and I learned how to kiss at girls like I cared about them.
You do it with every part of your face but your mouth.

The Touching

Soybean rust has taken the fields between Verona
and Madison, a checkered quilt of bronzed low-growers
and stubbled dirt whirring past open bus windows.
The pressure at this speed buffets a pulse over the heads
of sixth-graders sprawled in bench seats, held at attention
as a kid peels off his sock, sticks his webbed foot
into the aisle and offers *Free samples of the touching.*
It could be a kind of awe in which they are held
because no one reaches out. The wind barrels through.
And though last week he sat in the office for eight
straight hours after a counselor heard him say *Pussy*
and slap a smaller boy, here his bare foot is lighted
like a proscenium centered in a half-circle of pre-
adolescents. *Free samples of the touching,* he says
again, wags the big toe to demonstrate its wing
of connection to the others. When he tires there,
leg extended, and begins to feel less proud,
look to the carpet on which that foot is set twelve
summers later, to the bed from which it came,
the sheets in which it was wound, the leg it touched
and shared the night with, to the owner of that leg.
She is tired after their evening dancing salsa, the cross-
body Copa checks rubbing blisters into her ankles.
She is kind and has made things right for him, given him
a chance. And when, twelve summers beyond that, some
sense of loss pulls his stare from the back patio like silk
from a magician's sleeve, stop—give it another chance.

Because his daughter is there. She is learning a language
she deserves ownership of, in some way, and a right to draw
her own conclusions. The first tender rains have pressed
into the river basin and her only immediacy is the muffled footfall
that carries her beyond herself into the ring of trees in the yard.

■ ■ ■

A woman I didn't believe told me she'd *try anything once*,
once, a phrase I've since heard dozens of times with varied
degrees of conviction. I didn't learn anything from her,
which is a strange conclusion to come to after having loved
a person. Even so, I have learned that if someone
lets you in close, you have been given a chance. Even
when it doesn't feel like that. It felt like my heart beating
in my face when the older neighbor girl cornered me
in her garage and demanded I tell her how much I liked
her. Plumes of dust rose from the corner where she
parlayed my silence into hissed, repeated orders: *Tell me.*
How much you like me. I liked her, I think. I began to cough,
said, *A lot.* I wish I could have known how much more
we both needed. Years later her father, a man I had
never believed, showed up to my high school graduation
party and told me hunting, for him, was a kind of prayer,
the solitude of staring from a tree stand this devotion
he felt indebted to for giving him access to the universal spirit.
But it doesn't matter what I believed. Being put together
in any way is important. He touched my shoulder

when he left, said congratulations and drove further
into the century, divorce and his daughter's addictions.

■ ■ ■

The sock, now, has returned to the foot. The kids to their seats,
the soybeans to their season of drought and silence. At dips
where the bus slows or intersections where it stops entirely
the air stills and releases the fluttering bangs of kids
too young to care about being delivered late to their families.
Because it is late, and dinner is made. Everyone is tired
from their hours of trying. Someone falls asleep
on someone else's shoulder. Outside, it's all starting
to look the same: the slap, solitude. Spinning outside a cantina
on Park Street until dizziness has made the twilight drunk,
and wonderful. And the bed—how she reaches for his back
as he slides from the sheets. Muscle pulled from the hide
of a six-point buck, set to steam in the snow. A cigarette
bobbing across white acreage home, a bus tunneling past,
and in the back seat a boy offers his foot with a look as if
I'm not going to.

TWO

To Clarey

There's more to grace than departure.
It's other than what our grandfather

breathed into our mouths at dinner.
His house couldn't handle

anyone not inhaling it, a shell
of papered wall and patch jobs.

The first place he showed me
was the plastered hole

where he busted through
the bedroom wall

with a hairbrush.
That night, I leaned

against it while you
so dutifully burned

the needle with a lighter,
dipped it in the scavenged

vodka, pierced my ear
and nearly cried.

I begged you to do it.
How you could have been hurt

by tearing my skin might be
the answer to all of this.

Show me the damage
where you do not have a scar.

Give me your marks—
I will wear them

and not call them my own.
If I could mean something

because of what you mean,
would that be grace?

On Summer in Southern Wisconsin

1.

Let me state this as simple as possible:

there was a girl whose hands cupped to her hips when she walked
like they were holstering secrets.

What was interesting to me weren't the things she said
but the way she said them,
pushing promises through purple stained lips

and tucking them in,
breathing hue into ravines I didn't know
or had forgotten.

I haven't forgotten how,
in frail light,
what was interesting to her were the calluses on my hands.
Where do they come from, she asked.
Work.
There wasn't much else between us to say.

So this girl will say, *Kiss me.*
And I will because I won't know what else to do.
It is so simple:

there was a girl who hushed things into my skull.
My ears won't stop ringing.

Crowds of gnats clung to anything wet. It was summer.

2.

That August my dad lost something he didn't have
words for. I roofed houses with work-release cons
and blow addicts who'd eightball out of the crevasse
between their thumb and index finger.
After, I'd wait tables at a small Mexican restaurant
where they'd let me drink for free and glow off
my sunburn with people much older and much
drunker than I was.

I'd read with my dad when I got home
at sunup: magazine articles,
old movie reviews. He'd share stories infinitely better
than I heard or could offer on the rooftops.
When I sold my Buick and moved
east, I forgot about the girl and the cons
and the Mexican restaurant, but the calluses
stayed. I met a man named Flaco
at a truck stop who told me I had an old school
handshake and asked me for change
to buy a Black & Mild that,
for a reason I've never figured out,
he gave back to me.

From the Top

My sister struck her toe on the sunken husk
of a wide-bodied sedan. But I can't dredge Sugar
River or suck metal poisons from the pad
of a foot. It's not attention that invades my limbs,
tricks my body smart; when stands of sugar maple
are swept to bow at either side of this shared
adulthood, I bray. From an inner tube upstream,
listening first to assonance of veins through the skin
of my stomach, I hear her cry out and look
to my own feet, white like stones, cold and blind
to the muck of the bottom.

Float

We cannot know the stacked currents of the river
or how they pull even themselves under.

      We cannot consider tidal charts, signs with imperiled
      stick figures. I need to go; across is a spit of rock

and downed trees. Then the other side. Across
is where I can continue as soon as I catch my breath.

      If I didn't say how much I loved anything that afternoon,
      it didn't stop the fevered churning, the launch

and then release of limbs in water. It didn't start
what could have been an attempt to impress myself,

      maybe you, and fold into a clamber. *I'm a sinker,*
      you told me, I'm trying to remember when.

I'm trying to remember which one of us, between strokes,
is telling the other not to follow if you're sure you can make it.

Most High

Maybe the crumbs of a story are all there is to follow.
    Because to get from a flying creature to the dogma
of a child, I have to speak of dusk in elementary school:

my brother, sister and I throwing
    handfuls of gravel from our driveway into the air to whoop
and holler as bats dive for the rocks like insects.

Sometimes they get real close. Our neighbor James,
    after a bat flies so close to his face
that a wing grazes his cheek, proclaims it kissed him.
It was like nothing he'd ever felt,
he says. Nothing he could have imagined.

Much later, James enlists and leaves Wisconsin
to drive M35 two-and-a-half-ton cargo trucks in Kuwait.
    My brother files for bankruptcy then moves to New York.

My sister disappears for a while and comes back pregnant,
nineteen. She'd been collecting stray cats in a studio in Oakland
    and believed without irony
that Barack Obama was part of an overlord alien race.

I drop out of theater school and move back into my parent's home
    where I spend evenings watching the pink gauze
        of twilight overtake the sky from that narrow

strip of gravel wrapped around the back of the house.
    By the time my niece is born, my sister has adopted
a more tempered version of the alien thing,

something closer to Mormonism but more dangerous-feeling.
        She's going to keep Olivia out of school, she says.
            Her only society will be within the home.

I am gone by then. The next time I see Olivia
        she is speaking and walking and praying before she eats.
"Most high," she says, and names Jesus,

my sister's proclivities having shifted towards something colored
        Christian. I spend dusk for the next couple years
            walking north to south on the east side avenues

of Manhattan and retreating to the subway when twilight finishes
        refracting between buildings, or riding above-ground Queens
trains that filter between the islands like capillaries. I imagine James

in Kuwait, how he'd marvel at bugs and run faster than anyone.
        How when we'd finally go home
            we would marvel at much different things.

    There's an Easter I fly back and see Olivia,
hair golden and long, commanding sentences
        and asking play of everyone. A person. Forgive me

for taking her to the driveway and teaching her how to throw rocks
straight up into the dusking air. *Most high*, she says, and points
            to the sky. *Most high*, I say, and point to a bat.

Picture of a Girl

I am drawn first to her left eyebrow
where there is now a vertical scar

from a car accident maybe four
years ago. But above that

is the aura of stray blonde hairs
swept into a shimmering orb

around the perimeter of her head.
Her overalls are painted

in sunflowers rising from floating
clay pots. Her smile is the easiest

thing. It is clear: there is no gravity
in this picture of a girl. There is no scar.

At McKinley Aquatics Center
The Problem of the Gold Crown

> *Eureka! Eureka!*
> —ARCHIMEDES

Commerce is an issue. My understanding is that my sister,
single-digit to the world and in a roadside motel pool

tossed a palm-sized rock to the deep end and fetched it
with her mouth. There are repercussions for this retrieval:

the cracked tooth follows her into adolescence, the crown
into some kind of adulthood, both the rock and how it couldn't

be had figuring into the gold-flecked canine of a grown mouth.
The figure is sixty dollars for a month of this place. The figure

is my own, alone to tally laps in a pool. But in this daily
displacement all I'm finding are other men just as confused

as I am. So who's to do the math? The man who leaves his shoes
just outside the shower? The man at the desk hawking coupons

and memberships? The man who wakes, fist-scrubs chlorine
from his lids, blurry-eyed but within arm's reach of the world?

Because in the lobby the magazines splayed next to the coffee
list figures—men in uniform, men in charge, men of the year.

This is what it amounts to: the man in the shower goes home
clean. The man at the desk will feed bits of melon to his mother

tonight, coaxing her severe body to make it through May.
The man in the pool laps and laps. And listen, he could

hold you instead. He wants to. He could measure you
by what your presence does to the water. But he doesn't

know how. To figure it out he'd have to pro-rate memberships
into eternity, reach into the register and jangle around

all those gilded ways in which we are counting on love.
So many. Too many to figure. I'm so taken by all this living.

Look

It was beneath a slab of gravel-flecked cement
that my sister's fingers were crushed,

her earnest reach over the well's covered lip
brought suddenly
to stillness as if it had been a pupil

into which she stuck her hand without thinking of the price
so often paid by rooting around in the dark,

the lids that snap shut.

It was between that well's stone cover and the blade
of a shovel that my fingers slid

to hook beneath and pull,
to somehow stand and open a slit wide enough
for searching.

It was from my lips that the call came to look,
from my mouth the instruction

to feel. She did. And I let go. I was too weak then
to either hold on

or pry it back open. Whatever connection
can be made between that
and what's happened since,

I've missed. How my body's faults could be complicit
in her pain.

There are days when I think I've finally figured out
how to lift the weight, and days when I know

the most I can do is not look away.

Let's Intuit Something

Make it specific.
Make it Oregon, Wisconsin. The time doesn't matter.

And not because of that familiar trope, the middle-American town left
outside of time—although this is real—but because you weren't actually there,
have never been,
and I am going to place you there.

Since I have the choice, make it August. Make it the elbowed
weeds from sidewalk cracks,

sun-frayed and squinting through chainlink
at the laughs and bearing scurries of the skatepark.

Make it the prairie expanse elementary, as low and sullen
as I've imagined Frank Lloyd Wright's nailbed,
pressed into a fleshy, presumptuous paddle.

There you are.
And there are the swings.
You can taste the rust through the pads of your fingers,

you can phantom push yourself with a hip-pump,
you can listen as I tell you how, when he was just a teenager,
Wright made profit off the ashen slush of Chicago.

He became by placing new things
where the old ones had cowered to char
and it's held that he rarely prepared mock-ups,

geometric premonitions. Instead he intuited shapes into buildings,
improvised under a flatness like his nail bed.

We could intuit ourselves, but I won't make it that.
I'll make it fire,
which again did something for him,

destroyed his home in southern Wisconsin
as a servant stalked the burning halls with an axe.

This happened,
and I don't want it to be lessened by your love of *The Shining*,
Jack Nicholson bearing teeth and stubble through a flindered rift.
Don't intuit that.

Instead, make it this:
The late summer sun crests the hills now,

fields awash in an orange glow. Sparrows pulse pitch
through the dusk and I can tell you're tired from the way
you look at your feet.

And no, fire won't destroy us, but believe me
when I tell you this:

there was a third fire, a spark in a tangle of electrical line
that destroyed the same home, not too far from where we are now.
And he rebuilt it.

Intuit that. I will place you anywhere and form around you.

The kids from the skatepark have sauntered home,
the curve and impossible smoothness of the concrete
still playing with the vibrations of their movement.

I will place you on a curve, place myself beside you,
and search for the stillness in a country that won't stop returning.

Worth It

Of course, the votive candle—
anything autographed to resemble
   an expiring flame.
The simple fact of the 7 train
   or the kiss of a stubbled cheek
in cold. Your commute
   is none of my business,
but if I had to say something,
   I'd say it's worth it.
I'm having trouble with the idea
   of how something
should be about something.

Soundstripe

Set to the timbre and time signature of something happily
        confused, set to set some scene
and pitched in the hopes of summoning that shivering animal
in each of our stomachs,
our wrestling unfolds against a soundtrack
           my dad improvises. We tumble in the grass.

Lining the left of it all is the actual audio,
        coded just enough for us not to know how it trails us.
He lets me win every time. He crescendos at his own
defeat. This is all to say that I'm still trying to sync up

and that as a boy I was given power enough
        by the humming of a man to take him down
and put it all back together.

If there's nothing else I say, let me tell you we will wrestle
        things and we will want music for it.
If there's nothing else I do, know that dodging mounds
        of glowing snow in Times Square,

        I listened to the most violent music I could find
and carried that anger beyond the 3G into the bedrock tunnels.
        I'm not sure I've left.

But emergence is one indecisive letter
        away from being urgent and I don't know whose feelings
I've transcribed from the film strip.

        The question of what to coordinate with
always causes such a scene.
        This is the set up: the train pulls into the station,
            I step out and look for the stairs.

Shadowbox

As a drum stripped of its head
he inhales tempest blows,
a breeze wet through the back of his neck;

where once was vibration
comes empty the airy glance
of swing-minus-strike,

the pop and hiss of vertebra
just above the hip
to bend horizontal
and summon oblique, to righten and pounce back.

If you exist:
Are you sure you've made the right choice?
Your chin unsplit from swings magnificent.
Your face unbloodied in faux-knuckle splendor.
You're missing out.

THREE

Hands

On cold days the scars on my hands become
more pronounced, darker. So often these days

I imagine what my mother must have
thought when she found me on the floor,

lightbulbs in each of my fists, smacked against
one another as if in breaking them

I could make a kind of music—private,
imperfect, but sound. For a while I thought

to know anything you had to touch it.
The skin reopened for years in the same places.

I wanted to be something: a boxer,
a musician. Positioning myself

around things I'd play or break. What I've found
is the act matters less than what it leaves.

Twice

Twice that winter he fell on his way to work.
The frozen tongue of the driveway tilted

then plunged to a ditch. His tibia pulled away
from itself. It fractured the first time,

then shattered. Even after the traction stirrups
we attached to his boots, even after salt

and hours of slide-shaving ice with a garden hoe.
Twice a classroom sat expectant and then

emptied. But whatever lessons he readied
those mornings for the refugees to whom

he taught English—active voice, job applications,
the subjunctive—they didn't need a carrier;

Lida would go home, the mood of her tense
moderated as she cooked for her husband

and infant daughter; Armani would head
to the DMV; Carmen would linger

a little longer than the others then take
a bus to the lake. The report of the slip

would carry a web of cracks up to his knee.
He lay there, I'm told, for a while. I saw the photos

through a cellphone: calf wrapped in plaster,
elevated above the heart. Teaching in a walking

boot. The millennium was not as fresh
as it was when to get hurt was less of a thing.

I worried as a boy. And today I've learned
of his raise—for teaching excellence, a servant

of social cause. Modest, but these are his powers.
For a while I thought I could do something

with my legs instead of my head, and then
the other way around. The falls hurt just enough.

My breath carries into the night and I try
to catch the lessons hovering above the ice.

To be floats just there, below *have been*. *With doubt*
flips lightly in the wake of *that which we should*;

a flurry of clauses rises and then dissipates.
For example, that I did not own enough

to understand left me scrambling. For example,
that the ransom for a boy is a man.

Turn

Onto the barbed and broken backs of dads at the Rose Bowl,
emptied bottles, wincing toward the weekend.
Onto the salted and hardscrabble walkways leagues deep in the nape
of a season. That season, its blue forges and bitter nips
at wrists shoved into jacket pockets, stalled husks of trucks
too cold to turn over, the snow drifts lighted lowly.
The year my dad was laid off and couldn't get a lawyer
to get it to count for something. My chance
at college tied to a mare moving restless onto ice-hardened
roads. Onto Badger, Bram, Koster, rotted train bridge,
park for dogs. Lyckberg, vacant lot, frozen lake.
The shuttle we called The Crazy Bus rounding Rusk,
coughing the dull smoke of tardiness into the sky above
our yards. I held my head between my palms back to South Transfer
Point after failing a math exam for the second time.
Onto Wingra as the driver reminds me it is almost Friday.
Onto Sundstrom as he tells me I could be onto something.

Generous

So little is asked of the spindled figures
written into our mouths as children,

meant to be swallowed or spat, never
to be held on the tongue. One boy unfiles

his, separates the strange cord to hide
a section in his gums and spit the other

onto the neck of some girl. Or another.
Those other selves will, down the road,

reveal themselves as phantom transactions
like less imagined people in the margins

of card statements. There they live.
It's a funny thing how failing to either

keep or give can count, so few of us allowing
ourselves to be dropped into the simple,

revelatory care of that romance, to describe
the moon as a moon and leave it at that.

The Spoils

Winter in Wisconsin. Snowdrifts like the shoulders
of ancient and unspeaking creatures. A child wanders

among them, in love with the possibility of it all.
How the spoils are immense when there's nothing

to measure against. After a slapboxing match
with his brother, he chases him deeper

into the woods. They are hot with laughter
and watch their breath curl into the branches

above their heads. *Look*, the brother says,
and pulls the mitten from his hand. The skin

is pink and wet, steams in the air. He bends
to a snowbank with his hand outstretched

as if offering it to be licked and holds it there.
Look. The boy is rapt. He watches his brother's

hand hover. Slowly, the snow recedes. It pulls away
from the hand, away from the boys and the woods,

another season in the trenches of an axis tilt—
it goes until he is reaching for grass, then dirt,

layers of topsoil, water tables and stone deposits.
He reaches for the ruddy center of it all and that, too,

eludes him. *I want to show you something*, his brother says,
and grabs him by the collar. *It just keeps going.*

Even

       Even in the slate-cold January
dawn he boxes the brick wall.

       Puffs of breath. Awning billowed
below snow: YMCA on Midvale.

       I have been swimming with Jordy
for a week. Mornings we drink coffee

       and walk the eight blocks,
nod to the man who fights shadows

       before sunrise, stunts his silly
mitted fists against the building.

       Empty fight. Empty song
in the click of salted wingtips.

       He cannot escape his best efforts.

Heat

Val Kilmer has a blonde ponytail weave the same color
my brother's hair turned when he tried to dye it green,
before he came out or woke up in a ditch outside a club
in Fitchburg, Wisconsin. The thing is: he woke up.
I'm not trying to make this anything else. He rose to the thrum
of the highway and walked home. And the question of whether
Neil McCauley and Lieutenant Hanna are actually in love,
of what nature in the closeness of men Michael Mann wants us
to inhabit, isn't much of a question at all—
one of them dies at the end, is held by the other.
The only way this one ends is with everyone walking
home. Brother, may you always come to.
May you always come to. May you always—

Collateral

For a brother who sleepwalks only in summer,
something to toss around in: fresh bedsheets,

the sweat-through fabrics shuttled off to be cleaned—
I will give my nights. For a brother with migraines,

picket-fence premonitions of his own demise:
a spare bedroom in a sixth-floor walkup.

Nothing is spare. I remember how, in a New York City
heatwave, your vision double-crossed on an uptown

express train and a friendly stranger offered
his newspaper to sop the vomit from your lap.

You shooed away any care until it was,
you had to admit, time to go to the hospital.

For a boy with a migraine to carry his head's industry
away from people like a laboring dog

intent on birthing alone. What you produced
I can't say, though I know you chewed through the cord

yourself and pushed it out into the world.
And later that same trip, walking Bill's pit bull

through Washington Square, how you were dragged
for what must have been a block at least,

far enough to meet the halo of a shattered bottle.
We were only visiting. We were only putting things

on to see if they could fit in a few years. We have both tried
to live there and you are making it work in ways

I couldn't. For a brother to now own a pit bull
of his own, to pull kernels of glass from his elbow,

to rise in hot nights and wander—to carry debris
from a childhood accident across our strip-malled country

into an age of ownership, and for what?
And to admire the acne that blossomed across your back

before I knew to put my hands anywhere other than my pockets?
And then anywhere other than someone else's?

I've asked every night. If any current in your rising
and walking amounts to time, take it—for a while, for yours,

for the sake of whoever may be up and still dreaming.
For an entire season you will ask for nothing.

Do you know how long that is? For an entire season
your body will wander listless and locate the parts of its owner

that could only matter in health, outside, at night.
The city is doing this crazy thing this summer,

you tell me over the phone. The sidewalks carry the heat
of the day through until dawn. There are mirages in the dark.

That's not that crazy I tell you, pressing the phone
to my head. That's not crazy at all. For you to feel this.

For us to speak of this. For a summer with shadows
of sleeping selves. You know, for us I could give us.

You know, for us I already have.

Siren for Manny Pacquiao

> *"Every time he moves his eyes I know what he wants.*
> *He's like a baby. How you treat your baby, I the same*
> *treat to him. Every time when he sleeps at night, I do*
> *his hair. His nose. His legs."*
>
> —BUBOY FERNANDEZ, MANNY PACQUIAO'S
> FRIEND AND ASSISTANT

Admire him. He's survived the city, will tuck inside the songbird
itself and live too slim for a fight.

Light of God,
offer anything like admirers.

They walk where the boxer hooks up his heart.
They walk with a lean so hard that look:
there's Israel,

there's the land
periscoped over the South Pacific;
maternity bills, a small boy, a wide mouth.

I'm asking for permission to protect something,
to keep the holes in my game,

to show up to promise anything.
The camera crew sets lamps behind him.

Open the gym door into
his back, his shoulders,

his shape sliced out—
the light will come from behind.

Recognize our faces, afflicted by men. Do their hair.
Do their nose. Do their legs.

Following

The man in the wheelchair is riding herd

     on the kids at the bus stop
     and when he tells my father about the polio,
     how he can bend his legs

     back at the knee and touch the toes to his tailbone,
     all I can think of is how, as a child, he exchanged stares

     with a tiger coiled in the brush
     outside of his own school. There's so much more
     you don't know than you do.

     What's not to trust in that?
     I know that on the banks of the Mekong he sat,
     panting and bare, too tired

     to swim and too scared to keep running.
     I know that when the stars began to glint

     he held a cold thumb over his left eye to eclipse
     the moon. He's been on an airplane exactly once in his life.
     And he was exactly on that airplane—

     precisely in his seat, as sure a person as there can be.

     And here he is exactly in the center
     of the intersection at Rusk and Sunnymeade,
     corralling a gaggle of raucous, ball-bouncing children,

counting exactly each timid spring
his daughter makes down her hopscotch court and calling it
back to her.

And barely looking—how could he know?

Soon she'll be old enough to take the bus with her brothers
but for now she will play, eat breakfast,

sleep flush against her father's thigh. If what I know
is what I can actually see
then I know she will trip, abrade her face

on the asphalt and bleed.
I don't know whether I will bring cold rags
and press them into the cuts

or if I will trail and watch as she wails down the street
in her father's lap, headed due north of where I stand

now, a direction as certain as what anyone
else could see would they care to look—

beneath bowed ginkgos and sugar maples littering the street
with leaves in an early fall: someone chasing someone,

someone getting left behind.

Feat

Bluestem and prairie aster box each other out
for better sun at Valleyside, where swimmers

haven't flattened things with their wide towels
like sails towing profiled bodies across the still-flat

earth. A red-tailed hawk leans into the wind
and blinks, turning its head to look only

in the direction it isn't headed. And on the trail
that leads from the slushie vendor's wood-paneled

stand a boy steals into the woods, his heel brushing
a copse of ferns. There, he coaxes a snake

into an empty chip bag with a stick.
It is lean and brown, the tongue flashing out

like a small flame. He folds over the top of the bag
and shoves it into his backpack. And though,

on the bus ride back, the bag is stowed beneath
his seat and he begins to nod off, what he's

wrenched from when the snake punctuates
its hours of blind prods inside the zippered pouch

with a single, Hail Mary bite, is not exactly sleep;
he's been wandering corn fields at dawn,

parsing sense from thick clouds of mist
hung at his knees—he's looking for something

to bring home and show his family. It's almost gentle,
the way the fangs push through

the canvas and sink into his foot. Almost slow.
Imagine Achilles stumbling into a fountain

with that limp-legged hobble, his incredulous
fall to the water. Imagine him pulling the arrow from

his foot, inspecting its head as if it had been there
all along and should be replaced. Imagine him

putting it back into his heel. If in weakness
there is indeed some kind of absence, it is only

to welcome things in. The boy doesn't cry out
as he's bitten or shift the bag. He's lifted

from his dozing then put back. Barely a witness
to himself. This will be the day he brings

something home worth showing, exciting his sister
to a supreme thrill that sees her dance

in the driveway and be carried by her blind
and trustworthy feet. This will be the day

that slows enough for him to catch and know,
finally, its one possible meaning.

Apologia

By the second week of camp it was clear
the only thing I could do well was tackle.

And not because I was good at gauging
pursuit angles or wrapping at the hips—

I just put my head down and hit people.
This was before anyone thought it important

enough to tell me not to, or that there
were better ways of doing it. Each play

I ruined by dropping a pass I made
up for, later, when I'd stand up the full-

back and tear at the meat of his hamstrings
until we were both on the ground. They all

understood what I was doing. I don't
think I will again know decency like

what I was shown when Sam got to his feet
after I'd struck him and said *I'm sorry*.

Watch for It Everywhere

Jordy ended up as jacked and crooked off weights
as that guy in that movie who tears off down route whatever
before being nabbed—the route being the important thing,
because on it he passes a turquoise Del Sol with a bumper sticker
that says *Your Lucky Number Is 603571842. Watch for It Everywhere.*

When I started speaking in phrases from bumper stickers
it was less of a surprise to me than it was to Jordy.
Don't Drink and Park—Accidents Cause People,
I told Jordy. *Horn Broke, Watch for Finger.*
We took off on our own routes, moraines slumped
in rearviews like the shoulders of something
larger than we can speak about. *Death Is God's Way of Telling You
Not to Be Such a Wise Guy.* I could never be as funny
as Jordy. But the funny things were synapses
and when those left most everything did.

                              So there's the route,
the moraine highway, and Jordy's there and me
and God and we're using our middle fingers
instead of the horn and we're looking for the number,
watching for it everywhere. When we get into an accident
it's because Jordy strafes into oncoming, craning his neck
to read a license plate. I close my eyes as the car flips,
still watching for the number. I can feel something soft on my face,
like the flat-lipped leaves of tulips falling up.

Grace to Our Spines

I heard them say that Jordy could squat a house.
For an entire summer I watched Jordy load a bar

between his shoulders and back out from the safety
of clips and collars to crank them out, always below

parallel, in the center of the room. And so? I tend
to find things like this. Look, Jordy: some people

will not find any unprotected push. Some people
only find a God's parting—patience

and charity and *love thy brother*s tossed empty
and plastic to the weeded median. I was bashed

and being tailed but tried to net each flailing
virtue. I loaded a trailer onto my own shoulders

and could only shake. Only strain, still and astonished.
There's this shaking inside of us no one should have to

explain. There are caves within our shoulders. We could
all be there, all in love, good on the world and ready.

We could back into the middle of the room, push
hollow and staple each fluttering grace to our spines.

The Creatures We Must Become

At the bar the waitresses are in formation as if convened
    for the coffee and chatter
of a commuter morning in the din of Grand Central, their conductor
    a thin and almost gray maître d'
                reciting the requisite state of arrival.

First date ready. How could this pre-
shift ritual be revised to better fit the eleven-hour slur

    of not-so-subtle violence into which they are about
to step, the flicked pin and chuck of every grenade-
             grade stare and pickup line?
    The gazes and lingering grasps
at hands on check presenters—if there is anything I know
    it is that I must think

    of the rubberized creature toys my father had us pull from bins
in a brightly lit store off the square:
    women from '50's movie posters, half-monster

and stuck somewhere between scary and sorry.
    There was Wasp Woman,
black lips puckered at a man speared on one of her mandibles;

Jungle Woman swinging from a piece of vine with a stone dagger
    pinched between her teeth;
She-Demons on motorcycles with fiery mufflers;

Prehistoric Women stalking the professors of archeological
digs wearing tasteful warpaint and brown fur loincloths.
                    To be attacked by the Devil Girl from Mars

    actually meant subduing her
enough to bring back to Earth and collaborate
        on a cross-universe sustainability initiative.

    Your inability to see yourself with the 50 Foot Woman
was an issue of perspective: roughly twice the size of the others,

    it meant extracting her from the bunch to see her
in the context of the rest of the world,
                    which dwarfs her and is already too big anyway.

What these women were supposed to be was wrong and savable.
    As if being controlled were some transcendent
graciousness. This is something I know:

            each of those waitresses is my sister.
    The synaptic cost of saving someone
who doesn't need to be saved is an issue of scope.
    To remove her from this place to look at in terms of the rest
makes her towering. The world is too small anyway.

Anywhere else and the entire planet is getting eclipsed.
It's only a matter of time before the peak hour train sounds to board,

      before she stands up through the terminal's constellated ceiling
               and steps toward the coast.
Stars and scraps of blue plaster
    shower the station floor. The sky is spurred in her wake.
We are too light not to get blown along in her breath,
           eventually away.

NOTES

"For Floyd Patterson: A Letter" and "On Boxing" depict fictionalized versions of the boxer, though he was famous for his tenderness with opponents both in and outside of the ring.

Some of the italicized lines in "For Claudius" are from the King's monologue in Act 1, Scene 2 of *Hamlet*.

"Siren for Manny Pacquiao" takes its epigraph and some language from the article *Manny Pacquiao is Fighting a lot more than Floyd Mayweather* by Kerry Howley, published in *NY Mag*, April 2015.